Raven Of Isfahan

Poems of War, Exile, and Love

Mahnaz Badihian

TABLE OF CONTENTS

Cover Art: Pooyan B. Sadeghi 1997

This collection belongs to human kindness and peace, and Shirin, Pooyan, Mahvand,

Raven

Soak your fingers in wine
plant the sun in your heart
so we can defeat dark times

Come tonight
it's been long since moonlight
has waited behind these windows
to be open

Come tonight
so all the closed windows
old and shaggy
open from the rush of your aroma

I invited the raven
to come with the familiar music
from our country
to remind us of good old times
when that familiar raven flew between
treetops in our backyard
then settled on our porch while singing
intensely with excitement
as if he had important news
I remember the day you said
"War will stop soon, because
the raven is singing longer and louder
today."

That Street

I'll tell you the story of that street
with the long, wide, dirt-filled road
of many simple people
who gossiped freely
and attended weddings
and burials together

That was the street of close
siblings and relatives

I could walk through every house
and say "Hi!" freely
I could walk to my grandparents' house
and see my uncle having sex with
the girl in a red dress, easily

I could see grandmother weaving
in one corner and
in another, grandfather in bed
with his new wife, freely

I could see my mother was
pregnant again, easily
and I could see my brothers
fighting over nothing easily
and boys were watching
little girls grow taller, freely

Today that street holds

strange faces,
but my brothers are still
fighting over nothing, easily

Pomegranate Tree

Nothing will happen
if my pomegranate tree
forgets me
if no one remembers me

There are women
who will carry all my pains
on their shoulders
who will walk with my legs
who will fall in love
with my heart
and enjoy the stars
with my eyes
who will write my poems
about love and wars

There are women
who will go to bed
with their lover
with my body
they'll kiss with my lips
they'll talk with my voice
and they'll water
pomegranate trees
with my hands across this world
I am all women

My Father Goes To The Baker

I heard your voice
coming back from the garden
with a bowl of fresh,
cold figs in your hand

Your voice was happy, saying:
Boy, it's chilly,
but my lungs need this cold air

Moments later you left to buy
fresh bread from the baker on our street

That day I enjoyed going to
my aunt's house with you
delivering my American gifts to them
when I saw your happy face

Minutes later I found myself
next to your grave
in the outskirts of Isfahan

Have I missed something in between
from our breakfast that day
to your voyage for eternity?

Lunar Water

From now on I'll only drink
water from the moon
never again a sip of earthly waters,
not from the bloody water of the
Euphrates
with thousands of broken bodies
floating on it

Not from the Ganges River
with hundreds of hungry
worshipers around it

I'll fill my fists with
water from the moon,
to pour it drop by drop
into the mouth of the innocent
Zayandeh Roud River
in the city of Isfahan

Poplar trees are thirsty.

* *Zayandeh Roud = a famous river in Iran*

Sobhaneh*

It was early morning
rose bushes were covered
with fresh dew

Everyone was in bed
curled under blankets
I was awake and following my father's
rhythms around the house

I could hear and see the softness of his
moves
when he puts on his black leather shoes
and picks up the white china bowl
with red roses painted on each side,
heading towards the big wooden door

The door opens with a familiar creak
minutes later the same door,
the same footfalls, as father returns,
with the bowl filled with honey and
butter,
with stacks of bread called
Sangak just out of the oven

Father pours water in the samovar,
lays a *Sofreh* over the Persian rug,
sets out a bowl and bread
and a basket of fresh herbs

He calls mother's name
his voice is loud
then he sits while eight hands
dip *sangak* in the bowl one by one

Now years after he's gone
every day before the sun rises I see him
putting on his black leather shoes
or coming back with a bowl in hand
and a faint smile on his face.

* *breakfast*

Manghal *

That old brick house hosted
three generations:
grandmother, mother and me

My favorite corner was
an open space living-room
with three tall walls and
a dome-shaped ceiling
the second wall had a door
to grandmother's bedroom
covered by a wooden door
low enough so that she could
open it while sitting on the velvet
mattresses laid on the ground

In one corner of the living- room
there was an old red rug,
a pale, purple sitting pillow
that always looked like
grandmother sat on it
moments ago and still held
the shape of her body

During that summer
she would walk graciously
to the other end of the house
to pick up freshly laid eggs
from the chicken coops
Every morning she started

her “manghal” with a few pieces
of dry wood and coal,
where she made a pot of hot tea
and roasted an egg in its shell

Now after decades,
I think of her,
imagining that house
with an orchestra of grandmother’s
movements and voice,
precisely at the moment she
opens the chicken coops
and lets them free in the garden
the moment she pours tea
in the *fenjoon* and picks up an egg from
the *manghal*, with some ash on it

The eternal aroma of toasted eggs
fresh bread, freshly brewed tea
with a few pieces of rock sugar,
the kindness and love
on Grandmother’s face,
are lifelong delicacies!
Isn’t that what you need
to become a poet?

* *Manghal=metal tray with hot charcoal on which to brew tea*
* *fenjoon=teacup.*

I Lost My Shoe

for B

Of course, I remember
the day I lost my shoe
we were only kids
walking in search of butterflies
passing through
many plains and villages

We saw unforgettable scenes,
like people baking outdoors,
smoke and the aroma of fresh bread
made our stomachs gurgle;
moments later, an old man
approached us with loaves of bread
the taste of which never can be replaced

A few steps further
a woman was milking her cow
singing with the rhythm of her hands

We saw many colorful chickens
freely enjoying the grass
while intoxicated roosters
were chasing hot hens
and the color of their feathers
under the bright sun looked
like Egyptian jewels

We walked for hours

not thinking of any danger
until we reached a creek,
surrounded by trees
covered with butterflies
dancing around

We enjoyed chasing butterflies
and dangling our feet
in the cold crisp water of the creek
moments later a wave
took one of my shoes

You looked at me
to see my reaction
I smiled and said,
Now I'm like those kids
in the village with no shoes

They Killed My Brother

for Lorca

They killed my brother
the year of the revolution
because he had different ideas

They killed him
the year of the war
because he was in love

They killed him again the year
after the revolution
because he was aware

They killed my brother
on the streets of poverty
and homelessness
and they killed my sister Yotub
under the feet of demon men
because she was a brave beauty

They killed my brother
they broke his heart
they cut out his tongue
and choked him

They fed him bag after bag of heroin
until he forgot about home

They killed my brother again
and spoke of the dignity of his homeland

Again they killed my brother
in Freedom Square
and they sprayed him with bullets in the
public eye

But my brother is not dead yet
and they don't understand
the reason he will be
in love forever
he will be aware forever
and will protest forever.

Musk Deer

We're searching for you
on the soil where you lost your life,
the earth that smelled of evergreens
and daffodils, but we never
found an inch of your body

We filled our fists with that soil mixed
with water from the Karon River
in the city you were born and
made a statue from your clay
as memorable as Persepolis

You became a river filled by our tears
running through our house
you became young Musk Deer,
the perfume of your young skin
will never leave us!

**This poem is for my brother Fardin*
who died at the age of eighteen in the Iraq/Iran war

Saeed Will Recycle

Time will turn back,
and torn pieces of our bodies
will be sewn together again

Saeed will return
to his bridal chamber
from his grave
from the thunder of bullets
from Evin prison

Blood will disappear
from his lips
his coffin will turn
into a fresh velvet bed

Saeed will get up to return
to Freedom Square
to donate slogans to the sun
to the small garden
in his mother's house
and to the people
who screamed
Life is eternal!

Saeed Soltanpour, a poet and thinker, who was arrested on his wedding night and was killed later.

March 8th In Tehran

On March 8th in Tehran
women will rise up
with strength for the struggle
they'll remove their scarves
on rooftops chanting
"God is great."
as a metaphor for justice

Many women
with jasmine in their hands
will go towards Evin prison
demonstrating against
unjust laws

Women will write poems
about March 8th
about the lack of respect
by husband and brother,
about the laws of heredity

But there are women also
who'll walk those streets
with lost memories,
their bodies covered in oblivion
and a black *chador*.

* *Chador is a long cloth that covers hair and body.*

Old Matilde

1985

Visit me
and bring the aroma of my country
in your eastern eyes as a souvenir
I'm tired of these staring walls
and the creaking of Jackson's
footsteps upstairs
with his rap music all-day

Visit me
and bring tapes from
Shamlou's reading
who knew the story of
love, betrayal, and poverty

The bag of *sabzi** you sent me
has lost its aroma

Visit me
so I can wake up from dreams of
conversing with old *Matilde*
in this strange land

Visit me,
maybe this prisoner
of memory can free herself.

**dry herbs*

Turquoise Ring

This old turquoise ring
has a story,
which will never leave me

It belonged to the
one who tried to teach me
how to be a woman who
doesn't fall apart,
even on jagged days

Sometimes those breathing
feels dead to us, and those
in graves with few bones,
and empty eyes
feels alive

Wishing I could see
her hands again while
wearing this turquoise ring.

Hafez

Where should we go
to find what we lost in war

There's no door in this house
that opens to you
there's no telephone line
that dials your voice and
no city that hosts you

I'm far from your graveyard:
is this the art of exile?

We sent your body
to be buried in Isfahan,
so poplar trees
would grow from your bones

Now there's one thing
connecting us:
a poem in a book of Hafez
with your notes on that page
The poem reads:
Breath of the morning breeze
will be aromatic,
this old universe will be young
once again.
How tall are the poplar trees now!

In Marrakesh With Isfahan

for Youssef Aloui

It was me again in the spice bazaar of
Dejmaa Al Fana Souk
with beautiful people in colorful djellaba
with the heavy smell of black pepper
and hot spices for Tagine
and an abundance of art pieces

The smell of cinnamon sticks in
Djamaa Al Fanaa Souk took me to
the grand bazaar in the city of Isfahan

It was me again in the *Al Fanaa Souk*
in Marrakesh,
which centuries ago used as a place
for beheading people
and spreading blood
all over the square!

Now only snake charmers,
henna tattoo artists,
shops and live music exist.
It is Marrakesh where snakes also
understand Arabic and French and dance
to the rhythms of music

In Al Fanaa Square a little monkey said;
“Bonjour!” to me,
an old beggar kept repeating;

Marhaba, Marhaba, s'il Vous plaît Dinar

I was recycling between Al Fanaa Square
and Isfahan's grand bazaar,
with its turquoise-colored mosque
where they're selling natural loofah
with exfoliating white balls,
hundreds of art pieces
with orchestrated noises from
the coppersmith bazaar,
where at each corner
an artist is sitting
holding a hammer
a pointed instrument
creating ancient designs on the
soft bodies of copper pots and trays

Is art the language of all people
with no need for translation?

Identity

I'm used to you
my hands, hair and my lips
smell like your leftover cigar,
the heaviness of your eyes
has captured me

I feel the marks of your kisses
on my skin gazing at me

Amazingly the day I was looking
for my identity
I found my lost genes
in your smile!

God

God hung
under tree branches
under dreams of
weeping willows

God was running across
plains and forests, barefoot

God was limping
across the expanse of the exile
in streets of Tehran
an old camera in his hand
with a black beret like Ché

God was escaping
He was to be hanged
from the moon's crescent;
guilty of telling lies

God looked like
damp dirt, a tall tree
a lonely lion
sometimes kind
sometimes unforgiving

He was quiet
suddenly with one finger
pointing towards the sun
and another towards the earth

he mumbled something

God looked at me confused,
thinking I was a horsefly
or from the family of red roses

He threw himself into a valley
and with a frightening light
tunneled deep into the ground.

Your Share

Any face I see
you're in it,
any bread I eat
you have a share,
the dress I'm wearing
has your scent

I go to town
you're standing
on the roadside

You've filled this town
with your presence
with your footsteps and
your eternal aroma.

Fertile Soul

I give birth to a new woman
in myself every day
the art of multiplication
grows new buds in me

I feel life crawling
on my shoulders,
the gods of fertility
will never let me
stop being a woman.

Picture Frame

Oh, children of martyrs
with rooms full of
picture frames of the father
you never met

The pictures talking to you from
cracks between
stuffiness and regret
coupling between years
of bitterness
for no man was father to you as you
remember
not even the man who was a hero
looking at you from the picture frame

Children of martyrs
you climb from broken walls
searching for the men
looking at you nonstop from
inside those frames.

Rush

Life is a short celebration
and a long sigh

I wake up anxiously
not knowing what's rushing me
through similar moments
pouring through me every day

Love in existing form
will never satisfy humanity,
love so limited and materialized
that we easily betray, quickly kill

We keep searching for
lost pieces in our life
but in the end, we'll give up
and settle for an absence of
many more pieces

Such is life—a precious whole
with lots of missing pieces!

Lost In Ruins Of Baalbek

for Jack Hirschman

Milk dripping from their breast
tears dripping from their eyes
infants ripped from their arms
to be placed in immigration cages

Maybe that is why I felt lost
in the ruins of Baalbek
looking for lessons from history
between those glorious ancient
broken statues
talking to Bacchus, the god of wine

Or hiding in Pompeii, a burnt city
searching for a new poem or art
to treat my sorrows,
or wandering in the calm Bazaar of Isfahan
that welcomes everyone to the
the ecstasy of culture, art, and simplicity

But I know I was lost imagining myself
in the camps, hearing the devastating pain
of the wailing immigrant kids
taken from their parents

I was lost, imagining their scared eyes
in those cages, confused
not knowing what their crime was

The shock and anger of those children
seeping through my heart makes me
lost in the darkness of this crime,
adding up to the ugly face of slavery.

Stars

Stars have lost their way tonight
the moon is faded,
looking to complete its shape

I've lost someone today
and I know those wandering stars
stole my beloved today.

Sweat

Growing up in an ancient land
far from here
thinking I'll root there forever

But I ended up recycling
in strange lands,
next to the Mississippi River,
next to redwood trees
where Native Americans lived,
where I sweated with them
in the moonlight next to
burning sage under the thick tent
covering red stones

I didn't meditate with them
enough in the dark
while reciting Tankashala*

But I feel connected to fire,
to the wet ground
and the aroma of sage

As long as I live
no matter which lands
I end up recycling in,
I can connect to people
around me, through one theme,
that is "sweat."

* *Tankashala= In a unique American Indian ritual, while sitting in a hot tent with hot stones at the center and burning sage, they recite and repeatedly use the word 'Tankashala.'*

I Only Can Suspect

I suspect a night
as perfect as tonight
with a breeze coming
through open windows

The floral curtains
next to the painting of a lady
with a gaping open mouth
are dancing like
drunken ballerinas
I hear frogs
next to morning glories
calling to each other

The smell of stock touching
the green sheets on my bed
where a man, naked like a statue,
is sleeping

I hear someone singing from
a room I never knew existed
as if she had forgotten
losing her son, my brother,
her country and her youth

From the window
I also see the girl who died
on the street of Tehran
was washing her face,

her blood pouring
next to the poplar trees

Worried that I may
wake up trees
and disturb the frogs
but never find the girl
they shot on the street in Tehran

No longer could I hear frogs,
but I was feeling a breeze
on my green pillow
putting me to sleep in
the early morning hours.

Lost Moments

Finally, my life is calm,
and I'm trying to capture
lost moments

Now I want to know my father
listen to him,
but his presence is limited
to the bones he left behind

Finally, I found a moment
to learn from his wisdom
but he's too far from the basil garden
he watered every day.

Returning

Returning to obliterate memories,
returning to break stillness
trashing all bitter, harsh letters
we wrote to destroy each other

Returning to work on new poems
painting them, framing them
to hang it on the walls of empty rooms

Returning to make love with you on
the bare bosom of
grandfather's almond garden
without fear of being pelted with stones

Returning to escape with you
to the shelter of
all satisfactions not known to me.

Wine

What a fool I was,
thinking a broken glass
can still hold a
few drops of wine

Is it true that weak people
cherish love more than
strong people?
Or maybe the argument about
that last drop of wine
keeps us headed towards
a garden of oblivion.

Yesterday

I saw you yesterday
you were wandering
on an unknown road
your hair had lost color
your shoulders were droopy
your skin had lost luster

Where was I all these years that
I lost your youth and
the color of your eyes
I've not read your poems and
the years passed by

Yesterday I saw you
in the street of my childhood
you were saying something,
a story, a poem we knew

Do we realize all that we've lost?

Redwood

Let's sing our hearts out
for these ancient trees
and whisper our secrets to the ears
of these patient woods
with diameters of their heart
as thick as those untold stories
of enslaved women
as thick as the skin of immigrants,
who worked day and night
for a loaf of bread to eat
in solitude

Let's sing our hearts out for
these tolerant redwood trees
that can show us the roots
of many human agonies

There will be time
when layer by layer stories
will be told by redwoods
planted by Indians, Blacks
and working hands.

Dead God

It's time for our universe
to hire a new God
with more education
more responsibility
and fewer demands from prayers
Less real estate in every street
with no mortgages!

We all hear the demand, the revolt by
forests, oceans, mountains and the sun
asking for a new God,

A God who can run with us
in the streets of poverty,
who can sing with us
on streets of protest
a God that can see can hear
can run and read *Das Kapital*

Maybe the God we worship every day
in a mosque, church, in our quiet moments
is too old to see, to hear, to act;
perhaps his early age of a thousand years is
finally affecting his judgment,
God, who has supper with criminals
who plays cards with killers

Yes. it's time for our universe
to hire a new God.

Every Morning

Every morning before
I wash my face or comb my hair
before the sun rises,
I visit every tree in this garden

All the trees know a few facts
The same woman
will water them day after day,
the woman who picks one apple
from the red apple tree,
the woman who asks them if
the rain lets them sleep at night?

Not all the trees are happy
Some are moody
Some get annoyed
with cold or heat
Some are so difficult,
they hate being touched
Some bravely grow tall
even in the absence of rain
by now, I know their names
I know what makes each one smile

The man who sleeps in my bed is
like those trees, never talks
Once I asked him the reason:
Is it the rain
or the yellow color of the sheets

or the color of my eyes
or the size of my thighs
or just the way I lay down?

It's morning; the trees are waiting!

Confusion

If you decide to forgive me
I'll make it easy
I'll tell you how for so long,
I was confined in my solitude

And how I kept recycling in
confusion of exile
that I couldn't hold
onto those weary moments
calmly and clearly

If you decide to forgive me
for not being there with you,
side by side, day by day,
let me tell you about the time
I was lost, facing
a strange direction

I forgave you for being absent,
in those hard days when I needed
caressing hands and a loving soul.

Mithraism

I was born in those simple houses,
August or May,
night or day didn't matter
It was centuries ago
before Mithraism
before Da Vinci
created Mona Lisa

Inky fingers, disheveled hair
belong to a girl
who never dies in me,
a girl who goes to the river
and brings a basket of wet sunshine
and a fist of water for dead lilies

Sits on steps of Persepolis
to write a poem for lemon trees
in gardens next to the Caspian Sea
unaware of cold seasons!

Come Back

father

Come back to this house
and pick up nothingness
We want you behind windows
to wipe out the shadows formed
in your absence

We want you to sit around
the dining table and tell us
about your life
about your adventures
in the life you fed yourself
at such a young age
where you constantly
found and lost happiness and
witnessed human misery

We have time now
to listen, to love,
to have you
the doors are open
come back.

Subterranean Canals

mother

Life was a narrow road,
you were on your own,
standing tall like a cypress tree
on that rough, uncertain road
brave as your ancestors' Sandal and Bidel

You were the clarity of
subterranean canals
news of almond blossoms,
the memory of 'Isfahan.'

You will return again
with the birth of each baby girl
the world will wait for you
with its beauty, war, idiocy
and constant bitterness

Oh, daughter of Zoroaster,
come to my solitude
behind house number
24 on Mehrdad Street
where your loneliness
was an old carpet woven from pain
appear next to the Golden Gate
migrating birds are waiting.

Qanat (dates back 3000 years): a symbol of Iranian identity and national skill in irrigation. Sandel and Bidel are my ancestors; their children engineered the subterranean canal in Isfahan, and their names are in the 'Iran subterranean canal' history.

Like That

Like a pain that followed us
from childhood,
the same pain we witnessed
on our father's face
when money ended
before the end of the month!

Like an invisible shadow hiding
in the four corners of our house,
the pain of living in this world
with its many wars, many crimes,
many young lives lost every day

We return to thresholds of acceptance,
to doorways of judgment
hoping for a better world.

Knowing between us and destiny
there's always a hand
turning to stone

We shall add our hands to reach
for the light in the depth of darkness.

If

We could be different
if only it hadn't happened
this way.

If only there were no war
we could be sitting in
the garden house with red bricks
our father built years ago,
and I could see you next to
the apple trees,
touching its fresh buds
with excitement.

We could be different if only
it had been different and
didn't happen the way it did.
Our brother wouldn't go
to war to die
instead was helping our father
gather dry tree branches
to start the fire for making tea

It could be different if only
things didn't happen
the way they happened.

But things happened this way;
I moved to a place
far from our garden,

I left my moon on
the other side of the sky
and it’s taken me years
to find a taste for an apple
in the new host garden.

Yellow Rose

Is it too late to learn how
to write our best love poems?

We had all these years
to kiss the eyes of daffodils,
to feel thirsty trees
Instead, we wasted our life
on hate and complaints

Now we have to carry
the burden of bitter memories
on our shoulders;
ironically as we get older
nothing's different
except for our gray hair

What did we do with love
did we bury it under the fig tree,
under the yellow rose bush

Let's pick up fresh figs and
a few stems of the yellow roses!

Seeds

It would be nice if life could be
tasteful, bright
and we could be as close
as pomegranate seeds.

Straw

Like a piece of straw
I was floating on
the surface of the river
bumping from left to right

The river soon will empty
itself into the ocean
and the confused, beaten straw
will disappear!

Can anyone remember
the journey of a straw
along the river of oblivion

Mirror

One day all these mirrors
will be covered with dust,
no one can see the truth!

Maybe then our consciousness
with each footstep of dust;
will wake up

We're all far from the threshold
of reality,
from the doorway of friendship
from clear mirrors!

The Love Of *2020*

for Marvin Bell, 1997

I feel I have a lover
who knows all my untold poems
When I gave him my new poem
he'd read it years ago

My lover's the most critical
poet I know
he has devoted
philosophical thoughts

With poetic sense,
he sees through my dress
my naked body and soul
and evokes their images in his poems

He steps into my ventricles
Involuntarily
I hear his steps
in the expansion of my lungs
he's with me in every breath

My lover doesn't look like
anyone or anything
but I know him well

He's not my son or daughter
I haven't seen him in this town
or in this house

I found him many years ago
when I was in love with no one
I found him after I woke up
from a dream
and felt I was crowded
in my thoughts, on my skin

Because of his imaginary presence
suddenly took me out of my space
Thinking of him gave away
my loneliness
and a sense of belonging
lightened my heart

Yesterday when grieving
for my mother
was like a sword poking my eyes
it didn't take long before my lover
polished my thoughts
and drank my tears
because he knows love

My lover is not a woman,
isn't a man,
has no traits of my son
or my daughter
but surprisingly in my thoughts
he plays everyone's role

He plays his role as lover best

he promised me before I die
one day he'll appear
before my eyes
in my room, my house, my city

I believe all he says,
I swear to him
He's everywhere, always.

Persian Rug

There are many rugs in this house,
some with lines of poetry by Hafez,
a few with signatures of rug weavers;
some rugs are
round square or rectangular,
a few given by family,
a few I bought to feed my eyes,
rugs I bought with my father

Now every time I walk on them
I see my father reading news
and mother walking barefoot
and a basket of basil looking at me

This red rug in the bedroom has
the look of a pomegranate tree
lavish, magical
the green one in the living room
is like the Rubaiyat of Khayyam
simple, calming, elegant
a turquoise-colored rug in the hallway
has the shape of the glorious domes
In Isfahan

I'll pass these rugs as a
symbol of love
to the next generation
colored with more memories.

Nostalgia

I go from house to house
from land to land
from this dream to another
but I do not find what I lost
Something has been lost in me,
a nerve, a root, a feeling.

Maybe I am searching for
my childhood happiness,
or the joy of walking
in the alleys of Isfahan
maybe searching for
the loving gaze of my parents.

Whatever it is I am looking for
isn't retrievable
not touchable
not visible
not possible
It is a feeling called nostalgia
that measures the length of my life

Salamanders

I didn't exist
when the mountains, plains, and books
were here
and that proud evergreen which
will never bow for us

You didn't exist
when the Zendeh Rud
was whispering rhythms of sand
in the ears of poplar trees
under Isfahan's sunrise

We didn't exist
when the salamanders
were reviewing a new plan
for their eternity in this world

Now you and I are here
and they're stoning us
in the streets of patience
with freedom verses in our head

We're here
and they're penetrating
the verses of humiliation
and death in our heads

We're here
and they're choking

human rights rhythms
in their bloody fist

We're here my beloved
and every day
the bodies of evergreens
and poplar trees pile up
in the Tigris River
and we never asked what
The Salamanders said.

DNK

I did not know how much I love you
till I saw you shaving your face
fixing your tie
and waxing your shoes

I did not know how much I love you
till I saw your imperfect way of living
the open buttons on your shirt
your off-center tie and zipper halfway open
and your hair almost always half-combed

I did not know how much I love you
imperfectly
but love is not always perfect and
I live with you so imperfectly every day!

Testosterone

Oh if there were no war
my brother could come
to my daughter's wedding to gift
a necklace to her

If the war did not happen
my son could read Hafiz
and would be free from
computer war games

If the war did not happen
I'd still be buying bread
in my mother tongue every day
and I would consult
Aunt about my female problems

But the war happened
and Pinochet broke
the melodic hands of Victor Jara
and Shamlou was tormented
we all lost someone somewhere

War happened,
wars will happen because
testosterone is always alive!

Triangle

I am a triangle
with one side made of you
and two sides loving you.

Temple of Solitude

My mother was not rich
but she paid for all my travels to the
dreamland
she never forbade me from going
to the late-night parties with stars.

With her generosity
white butterflies would be let free on my
skirt on my birthday
her thimble was always beautiful.

But my father was more generous
he let me get drunk
on the beauty of the vineyard
and my drunken brawling
would bring reconciliation between
poplar and evergreen trees

My father was so open-minded
he'd allow me to travel
in my dreams to the end of this universe.

Even the day I was in the temple of solitude
and my enemies tried to remove
the sunshine from my innocent shoulders
he stood by me and screamed;
She is my God! I worship her

and that day was the beginning of my
awakening
and believing in eternal love.

Some Memories

On the ferry on the Pacific Ocean
on the calm blue waters
and the smoky, foggy air
was hanging above the ocean.
It is early morning, the seagulls
were missing!

Passengers with puffy eyes
seemed half-asleep
lining up to buy cups of coffee

This is the same calm water
that killed my friend years ago
I feel the ocean smells of her hair
and in each bubble
strange eyes hang open!

I want to stretch my
arm from the window of the ferry
and grab her long hair
floating on the ocean
to pull her out.

Some memories are heavy but
stay floating on our chest
even in the vastness of
The Pacific Ocean.

Silence

I love this colorful silence
that knows me dearly, and always
waits for my arrival in its calm land
the land of silence, colorful,
gravitating to forgotten memories.

Stern Grove*

San Francisco is a bit cold
in mid-August,
hundreds of people, some old
some young gather
in this grove, sitting on the blankets
lying on the ground
underneath tall, old trees.

The smell of wet redwoods moving
through the breeze along with the clear
voices of opera singers and the hands of
conductors moving as if birds flying
while dancing

Some people holding a glass of wine,
and some a coffee
the branches of trees are marching
with the voice of the opera singer!

I want to be the wind at this moment
and move swiftly
I want to be the branches on the tops of trees
I want to be the lyrics in their voices
or to be the dancing fingers of the pianist
so I can forget wars and killings.

**Stern Grove musical festival is free and runs each Sunday during the summer.*

Your Shirt

for Jahan

I came back and the smell
of your body was floating
in the house

The purple shirt you wore
left on the bed looking at me,
the shirt with the shape of
your presence
the amazing color of
your caressing hands

You left your undershirt behind
and forgot to put the
history book in your bag

I feel in these voiceless hours
you're staring
from inside your shirt still holding
your body's shape
and the wandering perfume
you left behind.

Side by Side

Can you tell me if we can walk
side by side and use this fresh air
together

Can we talk
and walk through this vast forest together

Can we wear the same hat on those rainy
days together

It sounds easy,
but we never can be side by side easily
together

Celebrating Norouz

We had to soak a bowl of wheat
and swaddle it in a wet cloth for a week
then spread those sprouted grains of
wheat in a beautifully shaped
dish and let them grow into a weed.

We would make little colored figurines
to represent us so that they could sit atop
the grass wheat;
then the mother will go to the
"Charbagh" bazaar and buy
beautiful little redfish to represent life.

On the table we had hyacinths to freshen
the room;
then came the time to color eggs in those
little pots.
My mother would never forget to put an
open-paged Hafez poem
while reciting her chosen Ghazal.
She told us never to sleep with old
clothes on the night of Norouz

On the 13th day of Norouz
we had to throw those planted grains
in any river or creek, we could see,
to have those old, sad roots taken away
from us.

Bipolar

I laugh, then I cry
I am from the North,
then I feel my roots
embedded in the South

I used to be from the Caspian Sea,
now I am from the Iowa River
I listened to music in Shour and Beedad*
now the weeping of YoYo Ma's finger
penetrates my heart.
I used to swear to love,
now I only swear to the sun.
I used to spare my life for others
now I only think of me and us
I think I am bipolar now,
a pole I know, a pole you see

* *Shour and Beedad are unique Persian rhythms*

Rust

I've been here too long
every corner of this house is rusting
a cobweb is climbing rapidly from the
ceiling to the spaces between my toes.

I need someone to wipeout
the rusted layers in my heart.

Yesterday I heard the cackling music
of my pelvic bone
then I put off the burning fire in my eyes,
till you came in
to arrest the spiders from my hair

Do you think I have been here too long?
I was here all those years flowers
bloomed and died

Today is far away from yesterday.

Rain

It is the fourth day of heavy rain;
The hand mirror I am holding
shows deep lines on my forehead and
stretched lines around my lips.
The rain could manage
to curl up in my eyes

My love, can you go back to the spring
garden and
pick fresh basil for my lunch, and
fresh hyacinth for the table?

I was thinking to take a moon bath
under the moonlight tonight
and caress my face
with your voice, like a velvet;
I was thinking to hold life
in my arms lovingly

Then the mirror falls on the grass
below the window
I soak my hands in the rain;
and I curl up my hair with rain
life keeps walking fast
without the mirrors in our hands.

Ferry

Midday, mid-March
at the middle of the Pacific Ocean
sitting on the deck of a big ferry
leaving San Francisco going north

A pleasant, cold and bright sun
shining on my stretched skin, and
the mild wind blowing
my memories away.
It is easy,
I can let those memories leave me.
I can hand them to the wind,
to the unknown destination
to the ocean.

Life is precisely this breezy, cold, sunny
short ride, accidental, and
I have decided to get along with it.

Do I want to be that large, black sea bird
which is dancing on the flag,
sitting atop this ferry, free
Do I want to be this ocean
Do I want to be this lady with short hair,
large eyeglasses, a big diamond ring,
sitting across from me?
Do I want to be older or younger

I feel in balance with myself

with my mind
I call it middle age accommodation!
I let the wind decide on my hairdo,
blowing it from left to right
from top to bottom.

Ten Years Ago

I dislike these nights
when people are temporarily dead
and the creak, creak of walls are alive
with unknown souls marching on the walls
and that antique china bowl
with red roses on it
still smells fresh with yogurt and cucumber
with fresh basil, grandmother used to make

That old handmade mattress
and faded velvet sunflowers on it
that one day held, your body is here.

My companion the moon,
with its gaze as long
as Alborz mountain
creeping in through the windows
and lands in my memories while
moving around like a merry go round

Right here, behind this curtain
is the station of memory
with an old plastic bag
that holds many old letters
from the station of exile to the selfishness
of my brothers, and an invisible
the handwriting of father on love letters
boys wrote to me when I was a teenager;
I dislike these long nights with

fat, swollen roaches finding a moment
to look at my face and see
an absent woman

The smell of memory bothers me
especially on the same street
that my bird died ten years ago.

Where Is My Lover

Why was my love with his kind hands
never born
and I lost the chance to nap under
his kind skin amid sad days

I have always dreamed
that my love with his smiling eyes
filled with gazelles of Shiraz
from the alleys of calmness
slowly stepping into the ventricles
of my heart!
with his breath smelling of jasmines
and his body filled with the
silence of romance
while asking me if the small wound
on the little toe on my foot is healing fine
oh and I suddenly feel like a sugar cube
is melting in my heart
thinking someone understands me

But where is my lover
Maybe at the time of his birth
with a kick from a demon
he died from the blood clot of his mother
perhaps he was killed for his leftist ideas
maybe he was murdered by clergies
or by accident
maybe he was killed by cancer or by war
or perhaps he killed himself

Now every day I come home
with a new poem about all the lovers
we lost in the game of cruelty in this world.

DNA

It was Monday morning, and I was passing
the big statue
in the lobby of Johns Hopkins Hospital
searching for Room 20, for an interview
with Mrs. Willis

She had a permanent smile on her lips
her hands wrinkled with red nail polish
Mrs. Willis looked me in the eyes
How do I pronounce your name, dear?
I said, MAH NAZ, the same way it's written

Mrs. Willis, with her MS degree, said I'd try.
MENAZ, Manos, Maha-noss !
then gently she changed her voice and
said, Can I call you Mary?

Marry? Merry? Morry? Echoed in my head
I felt like evaporating morning dew,
like a branch of a tree under heavy rain,
like a fruit just fallen from a tree

I looked Mrs. Willis in the eyes and said,
'But my name is the charm of the moon,
the name my parent called me
and the man with black hair,
dark mustache and brown eyes.'

Mrs. Willis was looking at me

with open eyes.
I said: Mrs. Willis, is my name
more difficult than
Deoxyribonucleic acid?

So You Know

for H

I'll write to you, so you know
in this strange land
I'm alive, and my blood which is
floating in your veins
still singing the melody
our father used to hum
in our mother's ear
when we were kids

Together we planted the sky
with all its wandering stars
In our brick pond

The whole world was our little room
that had a big window to the yard
our shared room with a corner for
father to read newspapers,
you to read Rumi
and for Mother to cite Hafez,
while whispering with her tired voice
and shaking her head

I'm writing to you, so you remember
those hairs you pulled for fun
when we were kids;
these days are greeting winter
and spring is planting
white flowers on it

The boat which was getting us
closer and closer to the Zendeh Rud River
now facing a coldness of cruel waves
throwing us into an ocean of separation

I'm writing to you
so you remember life was nothing
but the moments that grabbed
and demolished our youth.

Decision

It’s just that right moment in the universe
Tuesday morning, 6:30 a.m., minutes away
from the rising light and the dying dark;
frogs have laid their last eggs
in the chilly month of October
on plants hanging over
the cold surface of the pond

Now it’s that exact decision time:
the owl has to decide about his destiny,
whether to go back towards
night’s dark ritual or step
towards the brightness of the light.

Ismail

for poet Ismail K.

I'm talking to you, Ismail.
When was the last time you had a sip
from the Caspian Sea
for dreams to come true

When was the last time
your heavy shoulders
warmed up with dreams
while walking across Persepolis

Tell me, Ismail,
when was the last time
your laughter splashed on your poems
on those cruel lonely days

Did I see you quietly crying
walking across King's Cross
remembering your country
and the ones you left behind

Tell me, Ismail,
your heart couldn't take
loveless, loneliness, searching
for love to fill your empty palms.

Tell me, Ismail, your heart couldn't
tolerate life without
glass after glass in a feast of drink

when you lost all the loves you had

Where's this road ends, Ismail
Read me your longest poem
in the moments left to us.

I Despair

I despair of
the withering of their god
of the slogan " God Is Great ."
atop minarets
atop a trade center
and on the bloody streets of Tehran

I despair
of black chadors
and bushy black beards
with their eyes on our private parts,
which makes philosophy tremble

I despair
of our taken streets
of turbans
of black cloaks
and of the word ‘whore’ in their mouths
and the word “faggot” in their head
all of which smells of death

I love the flowers in the garden
that don’t carry swords or clubs
that don’t gossip
and whose breath smells of tarragon

Fill my world with flowers and greens
with equal borders
and cities filled with daffodils

come play on the banks of our river
dance on the streets
let the sunshine on the girl's bare shoulder

I despair
of hands that put veils
on the heads of statues
of covers on the faces of roses

I despair
of the sounds of guns and tanks
of images of mushroom clouds
and images of burnt victims

I despair
of all the sorrows in the voices of the people
of so much melancholy for their homelands
for separation of roots
let the saplings arise with their hearts intact

I despair
of the wounds on my mother's chest
and her last breath in a foreign land

I despair
of a world in which flowers fear the sun
of a garden which fears the seed
and its morning glories are
depressed at dawn
and we're afraid of falling in love

Tie me to the sun rays
atop the mountains
throw me to the notes of music
to my daughter’s enchanting voice
and to her eternal childlike hands.

What We Want

It is not loved anymore and
not comfort and warmth
not desire to jump the cliff
not wishing to see our mother again!

Why go through the pain
of losing her again
No desire to converse with Hafez or
Langston Hughes:
they are busy exchanging
words of wisdom together

But one thing is always desirable,
peace and unity on earth that brings
freedom and satisfaction to all

A Cruel Art

If I had the art of breaking hearts
it would be nice
Then I could break your heart
to use its pieces for mending my own
then I would leave you in your loneliness
with your cruel heart
and indulge me in the calm of solitude

Breaking hearts is a cruel art
I lack that talent!

If I hurt you
my heart will break
and if I pull you away from me
a bitter feeling will hide under my skin

I wish you were a bird
I would open the doors for you to fly
to the green lands next to the rose gardens
I do not have the art of breaking hearts
You are that bird!

My Lineage

Where am I from that
my dress smells of tarragon
in my father's garden?

My cheeks are as red
as the flowers of a
pomegranate tree
in grandfather's back yard

Where am I from
that my hands are the
the stem of a delicate tomato plant
and the taste in my mouth
is a taste of pussy willow
in my mother's tea.

Where am I from
that my dreams are as blue as
the turquoise water in the Caspian Sea
and every Spring
apple trees buds in me.

You know I'm from that proud
river Zendeh Rud
from the tall mountain Alborz
from the land that
raised Zoroaster,
the first poet on earth.

Keep The Doors Closed

The air is tight here
the TV shows the bombed cities
showing dead bodies everywhere
keep the windows covered
my heart will escape in every direction

No more bombs and killings
no more mourning mothers
who lose their children to war

Keep the doors closed!
Outside terror is breathing hard
the voice of despair is too loud

Keep the doors closed!
We are tired of war melodies
which never tell us that
the sun will shine again.

Death

for Bijan Pakzad

It's death
hiding everywhere
arriving at unknown houses
without permission

It's death ready at intersections
behind doors, sometimes
under the floral sheets in our bed

Death is standing in a suit
with iron cufflinks
or a golden cane and a
a sharp eye that stares at us randomly
sometimes is covered with perfume

It's death, ready all the time
carrying a handbag
filled with gun powder and bullets

Death is quiet
except for the moment he
passes through the red lights
with pride
walking anonymously
with medals and honors
on his shoulder for yet
another unexpected catch!

A Man in The Café

The smell of fried food in the café
was intense,
a man in a khaki shirt, gray hair
wearing thick glasses holding a cane,
each step placed carefully,
with him a young woman in jeans
with a ponytail, pulling on a stroller
with a little boy in it.

They sat on the left across from me,
the young woman talking to the old man
in a foreign language,
then turning her head and talking
to the boy in English.

She opens a colorful book
in front of the boy,
a paper giraffe pops out;
with the turn of the next page
her order number called.
She leaves the book on the boy's lap,
seconds later, the book falls on the floor.
The older man pushes it closer with
his cane and says something in
a language unknown to the boy

Silence grabs the boy
he could only understand
the love in his grandfather's voice!

Neighbors

I live in a big house
wired with security,
covered with rough fencing
enclosed with locked doors

I live in this city where
fear is hidden everywhere
fear of the police, fear of neighbors
fear of sex offenders
fear of a gun
fear of a virus and
a Sunday school teacher
fear of losing, fear of loss

I am looking for a place
where I feel at home, a place where
we all can leave the doors open
to the music of raindrops and
the chirping of the birds.

Apart

As I get closer to you, I fear
separation, then I feel
far, far from you
fear of my confused heart
breaking apart.

On Saturday and Sunday
I stare at your picture to review
your eyes a hundred times
and each time with a line
from your beautiful mustache
I thread a needle that invites
my lips to silence.
I listen to a voice that tells me you
will remain as a picture,
nothing more.

So I frame my heart in loneliness and
hang it on the walls of sorrow,
sorrow for all these human conflicts
Then again it is Monday and easily
I forget the content

Dew

Like an evaporating dew,
this moment we are sitting on
rocks facing the ocean
will be forgotten soon
even the faces of our parents
are a faded memory soon

No one belongs to us
we are free of belonging
nothing belongs to us
time is the owner of us all
and will decide on our fate
keep going!
the end of this uncertainty
is getting more visible as time goes by.

Drawing by Ario

Mahmag.org
Badihian@gmail.com

Mahnaz Badihian is a poet, painter, and translator whose work has been published in several languages worldwide, including Persian, Italian, French, Turkish, Spanish and Malayalam. Her work has appeared in many literary magazines and anthologies, including *Exiled Ink!* in the United Kingdom, International poetry magazine, and Marin Poetry Center Anthology, among others.

www.ingramcontent.com/pod-product-compliance
Lightning Source LLC
LaVergne TN
LVHW050933080826
845145LV00004B/1248

9780578527673